The Best D   Cookbook

Homemade Dumpling Recipes from
Around the World

Table of Contents

INTRODUCTION

Dumplings come in many different, flavors, shapes, and sizes and The Best Dumpling Cookbook will open you up to a whole new world of delicious dumplings.

From pasta to pastry, batter to bread featuring sweet or savory fillings, read on and discover how dumplings have shaped the history of the world!

- Dumplings were originally a peasant food. They were a brilliant way to make the most of meat, by stuffing it into dough and combining it with other ingredients to make a little go a long way

- Manti were the go-to fast food for 13th century Mongols who were too busy conquering the world to enjoy a sit-down meal!
- Chen Zemin is one of China's richest men, and yes you guessed it – the billionaire made his sizable $970+ fortune producing dumplings
- Gnocchi originally enjoyed by Roman legionaries were made using semolina rather than potato
- The word dumpling dates back to the beginning of the 17th century in the Norfolk area of the United Kingdom
- Cornmeal dumplings with turnip greens were one of former USA President Harry S. Truman's favorite family meals
- During the Ming dynasty, due to their similarity to gold ingots, dumplings were eaten during Chinese New Year as a symbol of wealth

You can't deny this classic comfort food has certainly stood the test of time!

So if you are looking to add to your culinary collection of must-have recipes then The Dumpling Cookbook is the one for you!

Savory Dumplings

Bavarian Egg Dumplings

These dumplings make a tasty side dish for all number of main courses.

Servings: 6-8

Total Time: 35mins

Ingredients:

- 14 ounces bread (broken into chunks)
- 1 cup milk (warmed)

- 2 medium-size eggs (beaten)
- ½ tsp salt
- 1 tbsp dried parsley
- Dash of black pepper

Directions:

1. Add the chunks of bread to a large bowl.

2. Pour the milk over the bread and cover the bowl. Set aside for 10 minutes until the bread has absorbed the milk. Using clean hands, toss the mixture once, halfway through the soaking process.

3. Add the egg followed by the salt, parsley, and black pepper and knead until the bread is a dough-like consistency.

4. Pour the water into a pan and lightly season with the salt. Bring to boil.

5. Moisten your hand and take approximately a fistful of the dumpling mix. Hold one of your hands on top of the dumpling and one below. It is important to keep the upper hand still and apply a small amount of pressure as you carefully roll the mixture into a ball-shape.

6. Add all of the dumplings to the pan at once, and on low heat, cook for 20 minutes, until lightly browned.

7. Serve and enjoy.

British Dumplings

Add these light and fluffy dumplings to your favorite stew and transform an ordinary meal into an outstanding one.

Servings: 4-6

Total Time: 45mins

Ingredients:

- 8¾ ounces self-raising flour
- 4½ ounces unsalted butter (chilled)
- Pinch of sea salt
- Dash of black pepper
- Splash of water
- Stew of choice, fully-cooked

Directions:

1. Preheat the main oven to 375 degrees F.

2. Add the flour to a mixing bowl.

3. Using a coarse grater, grate the chilled butter into the flour. Add a pinch of salt and a dash of black pepper.

4. Using clean fingertips, rub the butter into the seasoned flour until it is a breadcrumb consistency. Add a splash of water to help bind the mixture into a dough.

5. Evenly divide the dough into 24 pieces.

6. Roll each piece of dough into a round dumpling shape.

7. Place the dumplings on top of your fully-cooked stew and gently press them down until they are half submerged.

8. Cook the stew and dumplings in the oven or in a lidded pan on the stovetop over moderate heat for half an hour.

Chinese Pork Dumplings

Dumplings are an iconic Asian dish. Instead of opting for the take-out or store-bought version, discover how to prepare a batch in your own kitchen.

Servings: 4-6

Total Time: 1hour 20mins

Ingredients:

- ½ cup + 2 tbsp soy sauce (divided)
- 1 tbsp seasoned rice vinegar
- 3 tbsp Chinese chives (finely chopped and divided)
- 1 tbsp sesame seeds
- 1 tsp Sriracha
- 1 pound ground pork
- 3 garlic cloves
- 1 egg (beaten)
- 1½ tbsp sesame oil
- 1 tbsp fresh ginger (minced)
- 50 dumpling wrappers
- 1 cup vegetable oil
- 1 quart water

Directions:

1. In a bowl, combine ½ cup of soy sauce with the rice vinegar, 1 tablespoon of chives, sesame seeds, and Sriracha. Put to one side.

2. In a second bowl, combine the pork with the garlic, egg, remaining chives, 2 tablespoons of soy sauce, sesame oil, and ginger, until entirely combined.

3. Place a dumpling wrapper on a clean, lightly floured worktop.

4. Spoon approximately 1 tablespoon of the filling in the middle of the wrapper.

5. Moisten the edges of the wrapper with a drop of water and crimp together to seal and form small-size pleats to enclose. Repeat the process with the remaining wrappers and filling.

6. In a large frying pan, over moderate-heat high, heat 1-2 tablespoons of oil.

7. Add 8-10 dumplings to the pan and cook for approximately 2 minutes on each side until browned.

8. Pour in 1 cup of water, cover with a lid and cook until the pork is cooked through and the dumplings are tender. This should take approximately 5 minutes. Repeat the process until all of the ingredients are used.

9. Serve the dumplings with the soy sauce dip on the side.

Curry Dumplings with Homemade Dipping Sauce

These dumplings from Northern India are perfect for serving alongside your next Asian feast. They are way better than any store-bought dumplings and well worth the effort.

Servings: 8

Total Time: 1hours 20mins

Ingredients:

Dipping sauce:

- 2 tbsp olive oil
- 1 garlic clove (peeled and chopped)
- 1 onion (peeled and sliced)
- 1 tomato (diced)
- Salt and black pepper
- Pinch of cayenne pepper
- 1 tbsp fresh cilantro (chopped)

Dumplings:

- 1 pound ground pork
- Bunch of cilantro (chopped)
- 1 onion (peeled and chopped)
- Bunch of green onions (chopped)
- 1 tbsp garam masala
- 1 tsp curry powder
- 2 garlic cloves (peeled and chopped)
- 1 tsp ginger paste
- Salt and freshly ground black pepper
- 2 (10 ounce) packs round dumpling wrappers

Directions:

1. First, prepare the dipping sauce: In a nonstick skillet over moderate heat, heat the oil.

2. Stir in the garlic followed by the onion and cook while stirring until the onion is softened, for 4-5 minutes.

3. Stir in the diced tomatoes along with a pinch of salt, dash of pepper, and pinch of cayenne. Cover the pan with a lid, turn the heat down to low and continue to cook for 15 minutes.

4. Remove the pan from the heat and stir in the chopped cilantro.

5. Transfer the mixture to a food blend and process until smooth. Cover and place in the fridge until needed.

6. For the dumplings, in a bowl, combine the ground pork with the cilantro, onion, green onions, garam masala, curry powder, garlic cloves, ginger paste, salt, and black pepper.

7. Using a teaspoon, scoop the pork mixture into the middle of the dumpling wrappers. Moisten the edges of the wrappers

with a drop or two of water. Fold the dumpling wrappers into half-moon shapes.

8. Put a steamer insert into a pan and fill with sufficient water to come just below the bottom of the steamer.

9. Cover and over high heat, bring to boil.

10. Add the dumplings and steam for 15 minutes, or until cooked through.

11. Serve the dumpling along with the dipping sauce.

Dutch Dumplings

Pop these simple and filling dumplings into your stew or soup of choice. They can transform a snack into a satisfying main.

Servings: 4

Total Time: 20mins

Ingredients:

- ½ cup flour
- ½ tsp salt
- ½ tsp baking powder
- 2 medium-size egg

Directions:

1. In a bowl, combine the flour, salt, and baking powder.

2. Lightly beat in the eggs.

3. Drop the dumpling into your stew or soup of choice.

4. Cover with a lid and cook for 15 minutes.

5. Serve and enjoy.

Empanadas

New Mexico's answer to dumplings, these spicy empanadas are a take on the classic Latin American staple.

Servings: 25-30

Total Time: 35mins

Ingredients:

Dough:

- 4 ounces full-fat cream cheese (softened)
- ½ cup salted butter
- 1½ cups plain flour

- 2 tsp ground cinnamon
- ½ tsp baking powder
- ¼ tsp cider vinegar
- 2 tbsp whole milk (chilled)
- Flour

Filling:

- 2 pounds boiled pork (shredded)
- ½ tsp allspice
- 2 cups raisins (chopped)
- 1 tsp ground nutmeg
- 1½ tsp ground cinnamon
- 2 cups applesauce
- 2 cups granulated sugar
- 1 cup pine nuts

Egg wash:

- 1 egg (lightly beaten with 2 tbsp water, for glazing)
- 2 tbsp water

Ingredients:

1. Preheat the main oven to 400 degrees F. Grease baking sheets and put to one side.

2. First, prepare the dough. In a bowl, and using a fork, mash the cream cheese with the butter.

3. Sift the flour along with the cinnamon and baking powder into the cream cheese and butter mixture.

4. Add the cider vinegar and milk, and using the same fork, whisk until entirely incorporated.

5. Flour your hands and work the dough for 2-3 minutes, into a firm ball.

6. Flour your worktop and rolling pin. Roll the dough out into an even thin sheet. Use a pastry cutter to cut out circles from the dough and arrange on the baking sheets. Put to one side.

7. Prepare the filling: To a large bowl, add the shredded pork, allspice, raisins, nutmeg, cinnamon, applesauce, sugar, and pine nuts. Bring the mixture together, using clean hands until incorporated.

8. Spoon 1 teaspoonful of the filling mixture onto half of each of the dough circles. Fold the empty half of the dough over to cover the filling. Crimp the seams together using a fork.

9. For the egg wash, combine the egg with the water.

10. Lightly brush each empanada with the egg glaze.

11. Transfer to the oven and bake for approximately 12-15 minutes, until golden brown.

12. Serve warm and enjoy.

Four Cheese Ravioli

Once you have tasted homemade ravioli, there is no going back. Italy's take on dumplings served with a pesto alfredo cream sauce is bellissimo!

Servings: 4

Total Time: 2hours

Ingredients:

Ravioli:

- 2 cups all-purpose flour
- Pinch of salt
- 1 tsp olive oil
- 2 medium-size eggs
- 1½ tbsp water
- Egg wash (for sealing)

Filling:

- 8 ounces ricotta cheese
- 1 (4 ounce) package cream cheese (softened)
- ½ cup mozzarella cheese (shredded)
- ½ cup provolone cheese (shredded)
- 1 medium-size egg
- 1½ tsp dried parsley

Cream Sauce:

- 2 tbsp olive oil
- 2 garlic cloves (peeled and crushed)
- 3 tbsp store-bought prepared basil pesto sauce
- 2 cups heavy cream

- ¼ cup Parmesan cheese (grated)
- 1 (24 ounce) jar Marinara sauce

Directions:

1. For the dough: Heap the flour and salt on a clean worktop and create a well.

2. Beat 1 teaspoon of olive oil with the eggs and water.

3. Pour half of the egg mixture into the well.

4. Using only one hand, mix the egg with the flour, while using your other hand to make the flour heap steady. Add the remaining half of the egg mixture and knead to form a dough.

5. Knead for 8-10 minutes, until smooth. You may need to add additional flour to prevent the dough from becoming too sticky. Form the dough into a ball-shape and tightly wrap with kitchen wrap. Transfer to the fridge for 60 minutes.

6. While the dough rest, prepare the filling.

7. In a bowl, combine the ricotta with the cream cheese, mozzarella, provolone, egg, and parsley and mix to incorporate. Put the filling to one side.

8. For the sauce, in a skillet, heat 2 tablespoons of oil over moderate heat.

9. Add the crushed garlic along with the pesto sauce to the skillet and cook for 60 seconds.

10. Pour in the heavy cream and increase to high heat. Bring the sauce to boil.

11. Turn the heat down and simmer for 5 minutes or until the cheese is entirely melted.

12. In the meantime, in another pan warm the Marinara sauce over moderate-low heat.

13. Preheat your oven to 375°F.

14. Roll the pasta dough out into thin sheets.

15. To assemble: Lightly brush the sheet of pasta with the egg wash.

16. Spoon the filling on the dough in 1 teaspoonful amounts approximately 1" apart.

17. Cover the filling with the top sheet of pasta, while pressing the air out from around each portion of the filling.

Press around the filling to enclose and seal. Using a pizza cutter or knife, cut into the individual parcels. Seal the edges.

18. Over high heat, bring a large pan of lightly salted water to a rolling boil.

19. Add the ravioli, while stirring, and return to boil. Boil, uncovered, while occasionally stirring until the ravioli float to the surface, and their filling is hot. This will take between 4-8 minutes. Drain.

20. Lightly grease a baking sheet.

21. Arrange the ravioli on the sheet and bake in the oven at 375°F for 4 minutes, until browned.

22. Serve drizzled with the marinara sauce and top with the pesto alfredo cream sauce.

Jamaican Fried Dumplings

Typically eaten at breakfast, these fried dumplings are a popular side or snack.

Servings: 8

Total Time: 45mins

Ingredients:

- 2 cups all-purpose flour
- ½ -1 tsp salt
- 3 tsp baking powder
- 3 tbsp unsalted butter (cold)

- ¾ cup cold water
- ½ cup cooking oil

Directions:

1. In a bowl, combine the flour with the salt and baking powder.

2. Blend the cold butter into the dry ingredients and mix with either your hands or an electric mixer until crumbly.

3. A little at a time, add the water to the dry ingredients until the dough holds together. If the dough is too wet sprinkle with additional flour.

4. Knead the dough until smooth, taking care not to over-knead. Wrap in kitchen wrap and transfer to the refrigerator for 15 minutes.

5. Shape the dough into 8 evenly-sized balls. The balls should be able to fit in the palm of your hand.

6. Add the cooking oil to a frying pan until the level of oil is sufficiently high enough to cover the dumplings to half their height.

7. Heat the stove to moderate heat.

8. Once the oil is hot, carefully put the dumplings into the pan.

9. Cook the dumplings while turning to ensure they are brown all over, light, and fluffy. They are fully cooked when they are crisp on the outside and have a hollow sound when tapped.

10. Transfer the dumplings to a kitchen paper towel-lined plate to drain.

11. Serve hot and enjoy.

Kroppkakor

Enjoy these traditional Swedish potato dumplings hot, filled with salt pork and onions. Serve with lashings of butter. What's more, you can fry them, slice them, and serve them with a fried egg.

Servings: 12

Total Time: 1hour 35mins

Directions:

- ¼ pound salt pork (cut into cubes)
- 1 yellow onion (peeled and diced)
- 1 large-size egg

- 1½ cups mashed potatoes (cold)
- Pinch of ground nutmeg
- ¾ tsp salt
- ¼ tsp ground black pepper
- 2 cups all-purpose flour (sifted)
- ½ cup all-purpose flour
- 4 quarts water (as needed)

Directions:

1. Add the pork and onion to a skillet and fry for 10 minutes, until the pork is browned. Drain off the fat and put the pork-onion mixture to one side.

2. In a bowl, combine the egg with the mashed potato, nutmeg, salt, and black pepper. Stir 1 cup flour into the potato mixture.

3. Scatter 1 cup flour out onto a clean worktop and turn the dough out on the flour. Knead the flour on the worktop into the dough.

4. Cut the dough into 12 evenly-sized portions and roll out into balls, dusting your hands and scatter the remaining ½ cup flour over the worktop.

5. Gently press your index finger into each dumpling to make an indent. Fill the indent with a small serving of the pork and onion mixture. Pinch the dumplings closed and roll them in flour.

6. In a large pot, bring the water to boil.

7. Gently drop the dumplings into the boiling water and turn the heat down to low. Simmer the dumplings for 25 minutes, or until cooked through.

8. Drain the dumplings and transfer them to a bowl.

9. Serve and enjoy.

Lemon Ricotta Ravioli

Smooth, creamy ricotta and fresh, zesty lemon make for an irresistible ravioli dish.

Servings: 2-4

Total Time: 25hours 15mins

Ingredients:

Pasta:

- 1½ cups all-purpose flour
- 2 eggs
- ¼ cup water

Filling:

- 9 ounces ricotta cheese
- 5 ounces Pecorino Romano cheese (freshly grated)
- 1 medium-size egg
- Zest of 1 lemon
- ¼ tsp freshly grated nutmeg
- ¼ tsp freshly ground black pepper
- Salt (to season)

Directions:

1. First, prepare the pasta. On a clean work surface, scatter the flour. Make a well in the middle of the flour and crack in the eggs. Mix to create a dough.

2. Gradually add a sufficient amount of water to make a soft, smooth dough.

3. Wrap the dough in kitchen wrap and put it to one side for 30-60 minutes.

4. For the filling: In a mixing bowl, combine the ricotta cheese with the Pecorino Romano and egg. Mix in the zest along with the nutmeg, black pepper, and salt. Cover the bowl and transfer to the fridge for up to 24 hours.

5. To assemble: Using parchment paper, line a baking sheet.

6. Evenly divide the dough in half.

7. Place half of the dough onto a floured worktop while keeping the remaining portion half-covered.

8. Using a pasta machine, flouring as necessary, gradually roll the dough out to the thinnest thickness possible.

9. Flour your ravioli mold and cover it with a sheet of pasta.

10. Fill each cavity with the filling.

11. Top with another sheet of pasta and with a rolling pin seal and cut out the ravioli.

12. Remove, separate, and transfer the ravioli to the baking sheet. Repeat the process with the remaining dough and filling.

13. Bring a deep pan of salty water to boil.

14. Turn the heat down to moderate-high heat, and in batches add the ravioli while taking care not to overcrowd them.

15. Gently stir the bottom and cook until the ravioli float to the surface.

16. Use a slotted spoon to transfer the ravioli to a sieve or colander. Repeat the process until all the ravioli are cooked.

17. Serve with your topping or sauce of preference.

Mandu Korean Dumplings

These crispy dumplings are a lot easier to prepare than you may think, so get cooking!

Servings: 30

Total Time: 1hour 30mins

Ingredients:

- 2 tbsp sesame oil (divided)
- ¼ pound ground beef
- 2 tbsp yellow onion (peeled and finely diced)
- 4 ounces coleslaw mix

- 2 ounces bean sprouts (finely diced)
- 1 scallion (finely diced)
- 1 garlic clove (peeled and finely diced)
- 4 ounces extra-firm tofu
- 2 tbsp hoisin sauce
- ½ tsp salt
- 30 round dumpling wrappers
- Oil (to fry)
- Soy sauce (to serve)

Directions:

1. Add 1 tablespoon of sesame oil to a large skillet and heat. Add the ground beef and cook until the meat is browned. You will need to break the meat up using a spatula or fork. Drain the beef.

2. Add the second tablespoon of sesame oil to the pan followed by the onion and cook until softened, for approximately 3 minutes.

3. Stir the coleslaw mix into the pan and continue to cook for a few minutes.

4. Stir in the bean sprouts, scallion, and garlic.

5. Squeeze the water out of the tofu and with a fork, mash.

6. Add the mashed tofu to the pan and continue to cook for 3 minutes. Drain the mixture in a colander.

7. Add the veggie mixture and beef to a large-size mixing bowl. Next, add in the hoisin sauce and salt, stirring combine. Taste and adjust the seasoning to your preference.

8. Place a dumpling wrapper on a worktop.

9. Add 2 teaspoons of filling to the middle of the wrapper.

10. Run a water-moistened finger along the top edge of the wrapper and fold the wrapper in half, pressing the top to enclose the filling.

11. Put your index finger inside the wrapper on one side and make pleats. With your thumb, press to seal. Repeat with the other side.

12. Place the completed dumplings on a cookie sheet lined with kitchen wrap.

13. Repeat the process until all of the wrappers are used. Cover any completed dumpling with kitchen wrap, as this will prevent them from drying out.

14. In nonstick frying pan or skillet over moderate heat, add sufficient oil to coat the bottom.

15. In batches of 5, add the dumplings to the skillet, the pleated side facing upwards, cover, and cook for 2 minutes, until their bottoms are starting to crisp.

16. Pour ¼ cup of water into the skillet and immediately cover with a tight-fitting lid.

17. Steam the dumplings for 4 minutes, or until the water has virtually all evaporated.

18. Take the lid off and continue to cook until their bottoms crisps, and they easily come away from the pan.

19. Serve with a splash of soy sauce and enjoy.

Middle Eastern Lamb Dumplings

A Middle Eastern spice mix adds warmth and flavor to these lamb-filled dumplings. Serve with a homemade rice and yogurt sauce for the wow factor.

Servings: 6

Total Time: 1hour 25mins

Ingredients

Dumplings:

- 2 cups plain flour
- Pinch of salt
- Water (as needed)
- 1 small-size brown onion

- 2 cups vegetable oil
- 1 pound 2 ounces lamb mince
- 1 tsp salt
- 1 tsp freshly ground black pepper
- 1 tsp Middle Eastern spice mix

Sauce:

- 2 tbsp olive oil
- 1 cup Basmati rice (rinsed)
- 4 cups natural yogurt
- 2 tbsp cornflour (dissolved in ½ cup water)
- 1 clove garlic (peeled and crushed)
- 3 tbsp fresh mint (chopped)
- 1 tsp vegetable oil

Directions:

1. For the dumplings, in a bowl, combine the flour with a pinch of salt.

2. A little at a time, add the water and knead to a soft dough. Cover the dough with kitchen wrap and transfer to the fridge for half an hour.

3. In a nonstick pan, and over high heat sauté the onion in 1 tablespoon of oil until softened and golden.

4. Next, add the lamb along with the 1 teaspoon of salt, black pepper, and Middle Eastern spice mix. Fry until the meat begins to brown. Put to one side to cool.

5. On a lightly floured surface, roll the rough out into a thin layer.

6. Cut the dough into 1½" circles.

7. Place a teaspoonful of the lamb filling into the middle of each dough circle.

8. Fold over while bringing the ends of the half-moon together to create a dumpling.

9. In a pot, heat the vegetable oil and fry until golden. Remove from the oil, drain and put to one side.

10. For the sauce: In a pot, heat the oil

11. Cook the rice until no longer translucent.

12. Add the yogurt followed by the cornflour, and to avoid the yogurt sticking to the pot, continually stir in one direction to thicken.

13. Turn the heat down to low until the rice is softened.

14. In a small-size pan, fry the garlic and fresh mint with 1 teaspoon of oil.

15. Add the garlic mixture to the thickened yogurt. Mix thoroughly to combine and take off the heat.

16. Serve the dumpling on a platter and pour the sauce over the top. Set aside to rest for 4-6 minutes to allow the pastry to soften.

17. Serve and enjoy.

Moroccan Chicken Dumplings

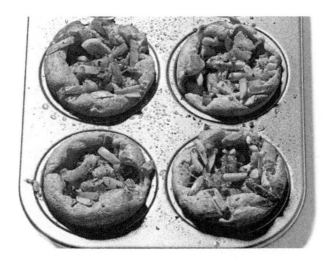

Serve these delicious chicken dumplings as a stand-alone appetizer or add to hearty chicken broth to enjoy as a main meal.

Servings: 4-6

Total Time: 55mins

Ingredients:

- Nonstick cooking-oil spray
- ¾ cup chicken (cooked and shredded)
- ⅓ cup slivered almonds (toasted)
- 1½ tsp harissa

- 2 tsp extra-virgin olive oil
- Salt
- 1 lemon
- Pinch of saffron
- ½ cup flour
- ⅛ tsp nutmeg
- ⅛ tsp cinnamon
- 2 large-size eggs (lightly beaten)
- ½ cup whole milk
- 4 tbsp butter (melted)
- 1 tbsp cilantro (finely chopped and to garnish)

Directions:

1. Preheat the main oven to 425 degrees F.

2. Lightly grease a muffin tin with 6 (½-cup) molds with nonstick cooking spray.

3. In a bowl, combine the chicken with the almonds, harissa, and oil — season with salt.

4. Juice ½ of the lemon and cut the remaining ½ of lemon into 6 wedges and put to one side.

5. In a small-size mixing bowl, dissolve the saffron in 2 tsp of fresh lemon juice, and allow to sit for approximately 10 minutes.

6. Put the muffin tin on a baking sheet pan and transfer it to the oven to heat for 4-5 minutes.

7. In a second mixing bowl, combine the flour with the nutmeg, cinnamon, and ¼ teaspoon of salt. Create a well in the middle and add the eggs, milk, and saffron mixture and gently beat, while leaving the batter slightly lumpy.

8. Take the muffin tin out of the oven and evenly distribute the melted butter between the mold.

9. Evenly divide the batter between the molds to fill no more than halfway.

10. Drop approximately 2 tablespoons of the chicken filling into the middle of each.

11. Bake in the preheated oven until batter is cooked through and the edges are brown; this will take between 12-15 minutes.

12. Garnish with cilantro and serve with the lemon wedges.

13. Serve the dumplings as an appetizer or add to chicken broth.

Norwegian Klubb Dumplings

Comfort food doesn't get any better than these Scandinavian potato dumplings.

Servings: 8-12

Total Time: 1hour 5mins

Ingredients:

- 4 potatoes (peeled and shredded)
- 3 cups flour
- 1 medium-size egg
- 1 tsp salt

- 4 ounces ham (cut into 8-12 cubes)
- 5 tbsp butter (melted)
- Salt and black pepper

Directions:

1. Bring a large pan of salted water to a hard simmer.

2. Add the shredded potatoes to a large mixing bowl.

3. Add the flour along with the egg and salt to the potatoes.

4. Mix and knead the potato mixture until firm. Add additional flour if needed to create a stiff bread dough consistency.

5. Wrap a piece of dough around each cube of ham. Aim for 8-12 meatball-sized dumplings.

6. Carefully drop the dumpling into simmering water and cook for approximately 45 minutes. It is important to ensure that the dumplings don't stick to the pot.

7. Using a slotted spoon, remove the dumpling from the water and serve with melted butter, salt, and black pepper.

Pelmeni Meat Dumplings

These dumplings are at the very heart of Russian cuisine. They are amazing served with sour cream and fresh parsley.

Servings: 10-12

Total Time: 1hour 15mins

Ingredients:

Dough:

- 3 cups all-purpose flour
- 1 tsp kosher salt
- 1 cup chilled water

- 1 egg

Meat Filling:

- 1 pound extra-lean ground pork
- 1 pound extra-lean ground beef
- 2 tsp salt
- Black pepper (to taste)
- 2 medium-size onions
- 4 garlic cloves
- ¼ cup water
- ½ bunch fresh flat-leaf parsley
- ½ bunch fresh dill
- 2 bay leaves
- 2 tbsp butter (melted)
- Sour cream (to serve)
- Fresh parsley (chopped, to serve)

Directions:

1. In a food blender or processor, pulse the flour with the salt. While the motor runs and through the tube, add the chilled water and egg. Allow the blender/processor to run for 60 seconds until dough begins to form around its blade.

2. Transfer the dough to a mixing bowl, cover with a clean tea towel and allow to rest for half an hour.

3. In the meantime, prepare the filling by combining the pork with the beef, salt, and black pepper.

4. Next, in a processor, blend the onions with the garlic, water, parsley, and dill. Add the onion mixture to the meat mixture.

5. Using clean hands, combine the ingredients. Add a pinch of salt and form the mixture into meatballs.

6. In a pan, fry the meatballs, taste, and season according to taste.

7. Divide the dough evenly into quarters and form each portion into balls.

8. Roll each dough ball out on a well-floured, clean worktop. The dough should be a thin sheet of around 1/16" thick. While you work, keep the remaining dough covered; this will prevent it from drying out.

9. Using a 2 or 3" cookie cutter cut out circles.

10. Spoon 1 teaspoon of filling onto each circle. The filling should be positioned just off-center. Fold the dough over to form a semi-circle and gently with your fingers, pinch the edges closed.

11. Repeat the process until all the ingredients are used.

12. Bring a deep pan of water to boil. To the boiling water, add salt and 2 bay leaves.

13. Carefully drop the pelmeni into the water and stir to prevent them from sticking.

14. Once the pelmeni float to the surface of the water, cook for an additional 10 minutes.

15. Using a slotted spoon, remove the pelmeni and drain.

16. Pour melted butter over the top of the dumplings, gently stirring to coat.

17. Serve with sour cream and garnish with fresh parsley.

Potato-Cheese Filled Pierogies

These delightful dumplings hail from Eastern Europe, where they are prepared with a savory or sweet filling.

Servings: 8-10

Total Time: 2hours 10mins

Ingredients:

Filling:

- 1 medium-size onion (peeled and diced)
- Oil
- 6 large-size red-skinned potatoes (peeled and halved)
- 4-6 ounces Cheddar cheese (shredded)
- Salt and white pepper (to season)
- ½ cup dense cottage cheese

Dough:

- 4½ cups all-purpose flour
- ½ cup vegetable oil
- 1 cup whole milk (room temperature)
- 1 cup water (boiling)
- 1 tsp salt

Directions:

1. For the filling. Sauté the onions in oil until softened.

2. In a pot, boil the potatoes until fork-tender. Drain.

3. While the potatoes are hot, stir in the cheese. Cover the pot with a lid and allow to stand for 60 seconds until the cheese is entirely melted.

4. Next, stir in the onions and using a potato masher, mash the mixture until lump-free and smooth. Season with salt and pepper.

5. With a clean piece of cheesecloth, squeeze out any moisture from the cottage cheese.

6. Stir the cottage cheese into the potato-onion mixture — season to taste.

7. For the dough: In a bowl, mix the flour with the vegetable oil, milk, water, and salt and knead until smooth dough. Set aside to rest for ½ -1 hour.

8. Roll the dough out until extremely thin. Cut the dough into even (2x2") squares. You should yield around 80-100 squares.

9. Spoon approximately 1 tablespoon of the filling in the middle of each square.

10. Carefully fold the dough to create a triangle and pinch the edges to cover and seal in the fillings.

11. Bring a pot of water to the boil.

12. Carefully drop the triangles into the boiling water. They are cooked when they float to the surface of the water; this will take 60-90 seconds.

13. Using a slotted spoon, remove the pierogies from the boiling water.

14. Serve and enjoy.

Poğaça

Turkish feta dumplings are the perfect breakfast or brunch snack. There are lots of variations for this type of dumpling, and this particular recipe is easy peasy.

Servings: 4

Total Time: 35mins

Ingredients:

- 2 cups flour
- 2 cups plain yogurt
- ¾ cup butter (melted)

- ¼ tsp sugar
- 2 tsp baking powder
- ⅓ cup feta cheese (crumbled)
- 2 egg yolks
- 2 tbsp sesame seeds (chopped)
- Salt (to taste)

Directions:

1. In a bowl, mix the flour with the yogurt, butter, sugar, baking powder, and feta. Knead to create a dough. You should aim for a non-sticky and pliable dough.

2. Roll the dough out into balls the size of apricots.

3. Flip, gently press and flatten each ball.

4. Arrange the balls on a greased baking sheet.

5. Brush each ball with egg yolk and scatter with sesame seeds.

6. Bake in the oven for half an hour at 355 degrees F until golden brown.

7. Serve and enjoy.

Pork Momos

These Asian steamed dumplings filled with pork and seasoned with herbs and warm ginger, are one of Nepal's most popular dishes.

Servings: 4-6

Total Time: 1hour 20mins

Ingredients:

- 7 ounces plain flour
- Pinch of salt
- 5 tsp sunflower oil

Filling:

- 5¼ ounces lean pork mince
- 2 cloves of garlic (peeled and finely chopped)
- 1 small-size onion (peeled and finely chopped)
- 2 spring onions (finely chopped)
- 2 green chilies (finely chopped)
- 1 tbsp coriander leaves (finely chopped)
- 1 tsp ginger (grated)
- Salt (to season)

Sauce:

- 50ml soy sauce
- 1 green chili (chopped)
- 2 spring onions (chopped)
- 2 tsp ginger (grated)
- 1 tsp sugar
- 2 tbsp water

Directions:

1. To make the dough, tip the flour along with a pinch of salt into a bowl. Add the oil to the flour and combine well with your hands. Slowly add 100ml water and knead the dough

until it is stretchy. Cover with cling film and leave the dough to rest.

2. Add the pork, garlic, onion, spring onions, green chilies, coriander leaves, and grated ginger to a bowl. Season with salt and with a clean hand, thoroughly combine.

3. Divide the dough into 20 balls, ideally weighing ½ an ounce each.

4. Lightly dust your work surface with flour.

5. Using a rolling pin, roll the balls into thin circles.

6. Spoon approximately 1 teaspoon of the filling into the middle of each circle. Using your thumb and forefinger, pinch the edge of the dough into a fold.

7. Continue pinching along the edge of the dough circles and work your wall all the way around.

8. Bring all of the pinched edges of the circle together to enclose the filling and carefully twist the top to seal. Repeat the process with the remaining dough and filling mixture.

9. Fill your bamboo steam with water, and using parchment paper, layer the base — pierce holes in the paper.

10. In batches of 2 or 3, place the pork momos on the parchment paper and steam for approximately 10 minutes. The momos, when sufficiently cooked, should appear transparent, and not sticky.

11. Keep the momos warm as you continue steaming.

12. In the meantime, combine the soy sauce with the green chili, spring onions, ginger, and sugar in a bowl. Stir in 2 tablespoons of water and serve with the pork momos.

Ricotta Gnocchi with Homemade Gorgonzola Cream Sauce

These delicious Italian dumplings are made with buffalo ricotta rather than potato. Buon Appetito!

Servings: 6-8

Total Time: 8hours 40mins

Ingredients:

- 2 pounds buffalo ricotta
- 1 medium-size egg

- Yolk of 1 medium egg
- ⅔ cup all-purpose flour
- 1 tbsp salt
- ¼ tsp freshly ground black pepper
- Zest of ½ a lemon

Gorgonzola cream sauce:

- 2 tbsp olive oil
- ¼ cup onion (peeled and minced)
- 2 garlic cloves (peeled and minced)
- ½ cup white wine
- 2 cups 35% cream
- Pinch of salt
- Dash of white pepper
- 2 ounces gorgonzola
- 1 tbsp chives (minced)

Directions:

1. Under cold running water, rinse a sheet of cheesecloth. Squeeze dry and use it to line a strainer.

2. Place the strainer over a mixing bowl. Add the buffalo ricotta, cover, and chill in the fridge overnight.

3. The following morning, discard the liquid, clean and dry the bowl and add the ricotta.

4. Press down gently on the mound to create a well.

5. Add the egg followed by the yolk and gently combine using clean hands. Add the lemon zest, salt, and black pepper. Mix gently to combine. The dough needs to be slightly sticky to the touch, if it is too sticky and wet, add more flour in small amounts.

6. Dust a clean work surface with flour and working in batches of one handful at a time, roll the dough into a ¾" wide log.

7. Flour a knife and at an angle, trim the end of the log. Still, on an angle, slice the roll into 1" long pieces.

8. Transfer the gnocchi to a clean, lightly-floured baking sheet.

9. Bring a deep saucepan of salty water to a fast boil.

10. Add the gnocchi and gently stir to prevent sticking.

11. As the gnocchi float to the surface of the water, after a couple of minutes, take them out of the pan using a slotted

spoon. Place the gnocchi on a baking sheet and set to one side to cool.

12. For the sauce: In a deep pan, heat the oil.

13. Add the onions to the pan and sauté for 4-5 minutes, until wilted.

14. Next, add the garlic and cook for an addition 60 seconds.

15. Deglaze the pan with the white wine, until a syrup-like consistency.

16. Pour in the cream and stir to combine. Bring to a simmer and lightly season.

17. Crumble the cheese into the sauce, stirring until combined.

18. Add the chives, taste, and season. Do not reduce the sauce.

19. Gently fold the gnocchi into the gorgonzola cream sauce until combined and heated through.

20. Serve and enjoy.

Samosa

Spicy filled and fried dumplings, samosas, are the perfect side for an Asian inspired meal.

Servings: 16

Total Time: 55mins

Ingredients:

- 1 cup all-purpose flour
- ½ tsp salt
- 2 tbsp oil
- ¼ tsp ajowan caraway
- ¼ cup water

Filling:

- 1 pound potatoes (boiled, peeled and mashed)
- ½ tsp salt
- 1.2 tsp chili powder
- ½ tsp dry mango powder
- ½ tsp garam masala
- 1-2 green chilis (finely chopped)
- ½ tsp ginger (crushed)
- ½ cup green peas (boiled)
- 1 tbsp cashews (chopped)
- 1 tbsp raisins
- 1 tbsp coriander (finely chopped)
- Vegetable oil (to fry)

Directions:

1. For the samosa: In a bowl, combine the flour, salt, oil, and ajowan caraway. Add the water a drop at a time. Pat and knead thoroughly several times to create a soft and pliable dough.

2. Cover the dough with a clean and moist muslin cloth and put aside for approximately 15 minutes.

3. For the filling: In a mixing bowl, add the mashed potato, salt, chili powder, mango powder, garam masala, green chilis, and ginger, and mix thoroughly.

4. Next, add the peas, cashews, and raisins and mix to combine.

5. Add the coriander and set to one side.

6. Form the dough into small rolls and roll out into a 4-5" diameter circle.

7. Cut into 2 portions like a semi-circle.

8. Take one of the semi-circles and fold it into a cone shape. You will need to add water while you do this.

9. Fill the cone with a spoonful of the filling and seal the third side with a splash of water.

10. Heat the oil in a deep pot or frying pan and deep fry over a moderate flame until golden.

Shrimp and Ginger Siu Mai Dumplings

These traditional dumplings originate from Huhhot in China. They are generally served as a dim sum snack.

Servings: 36

Total Time: 1hour 10mins

Ingredients:

Filling:

- 1 pound shrimp (shelled and deveined)
- ½ pound ground pork
- 1 green onion (peeled and finely chopped)
- 3 garlic cloves (peeled and minced)
- 1 (2") piece fresh ginger (grated)
- 2 egg whites
- 2 tsp cornstarch
- Freshly squeezed juice of ½ lemon
- 1 tbsp low-sodium soy sauce
- 1 tbsp sesame oil
- ¼ tsp salt
- ¼ tsp freshly ground black pepper

Wrappers:

- 1 (10 ounce) packet round wonton wrappers
- Canola oil (to brush the steamer)
- Savoy cabbage (to line the steamer)
- Soy sauce (for dipping)

Directions:

1. For the filling: Add all the filling ingredients apart from the seasoning to a food processor (shrimp, pork, onion, cloves, ginger, egg whites, cornstarch, lemon juice, soy sauce, and sesame oil) and on the pulse setting, process until partially smooth. The consistency should have some texture and not be a puree. Season with salt and black pepper.

2. Take a wonton wrapper and hold it in your hand.

3. Dip a spoon in cold water. Drop 1 tbsp of the shrimp filling into the middle of the wrapper. Carefully gather the edges of the wonton wrapper up around the shrimp filling, and gently squeeze the sides together to naturally pleat, and leave the filling a little exposed. Tap the dumpling on a work surface, so the base is flat and the wrapper stands upright.

4. Repeat the process until you have assembled 36 portions.

5. Lightly brush the bottom of 10" bamboo steamer with canola oil before lining it with cabbage leaves.

6. Stand the dumplings upright in the bamboo steamer. They must be in a single layer and not touching one another. Aim to work in batches of 12.

7. Bring between 1 and 2" of water to boil in a pan.

8. Set the steamer over the pan and cover with the steamer lid.

9. Steam the wrapper for 10-12 minutes or until the shrimp filling is firm to the touch, and the seafood is cooked through.

10. Serve while still in the steamer basket with a side of soy sauce for dipping.

Sicilian Bread Dumplings

This Sicilian-style take on gnocchi uses bread instead of potato and is served with a tomato and red wine sauce.

Servings: 6

Total Time: 40mins

Ingredients:

Dumplings:

- 3 cups day old, crustless white bread (cut into cubes)
- 1½ cups milk

- 1 egg (lightly beaten)
- ¼ cup flat-leaf parsley (chopped)
- ¼ cup basil (chopped)
- ½ cup Pecorino Romano cheese (grated)
- ¾ cup flour
- ¾ tsp kosher salt
- ¼ tsp freshly ground black pepper

Sauce:

- 1 (28 ounce) can whole Italian plum tomatoes
- 1 tbsp olive oil
- ¼ pound pancetta (diced)
- 6 cloves of garlic (peeled and sliced)
- 1 onion (peeled and finely diced)
- ¼ tsp red pepper flakes
- ½ tsp fresh oregano
- ½ cup red wine
- ½ cup water
- Salt and freshly ground black pepper
- ¼ cup basil (chopped)
- 3 tbsp Pecorino Romano cheese (grated)
- 2 tbsp parsley (chopped)

Directions:

1. In a bowl, soak the bread in the milk until softened.

2. Squeeze out as much milk as you can from the bread and discard the milk.

3. Add the egg, parsley, and basil, followed by the grated cheese, flour, kosher salt, and black pepper to the bread. Mix well to create a dough. You may need to add more flour if necessary while taking care not to add too much or to overwork.

4. Turn the dough out onto a lightly floured worktop and pat the dough into a ¼" thick rectangle.

5. Cut the dough into ½-¾" squares. Make a small indentation in each square using your thumb.

6. Arrange on baking trays and put to one side while you prepare the sauce.

7. Drain the juice from the canned tomatoes, and reserve. With your hand, crush the tomatoes into a mixing bowl.

8. In a frying pan, heat the oil.

9. Add the pancetta to the oil and sauté until starting to brown.

10. Add the garlic along with the onion and red pepper flakes. Sauté until the garlic is fragrant and the onion softens.

11. Next, add the oregano along with the tomatoes, and cook until the tomatoes start to brown.

12. Deglaze the pan with red wine and cook until the liquid reduces by 50 percent.

13. Add the tomato juice set aside earlier, followed by the water, and simmer until the mixture thickens - season.

14. In the meantime, add the dumplings, in batches, to boiling salted water.

15. Once the dumplings rise to the surface, cook for 60 seconds before removing from the water using a slotted spoon. Transfer to a bowl. Add a drop of sauce and toss to coat evenly. Repeat the process until the ingredients are used.

16. Garnish with basil, cheese, and parsley.

Suet Dumplings

In lots of areas in the UK, suet dumplings are added to a wide range of stews and pottages.

Servings: 8

Total Time: 30mins

Ingredients:

- 4 ounces self-raising flour
- 2 ounces suet
- 2-3 tablespoons cold water
- Salt and black pepper (to taste)

Directions:

1. In a bowl, combine the self-raising flour with the suet.

2. A little at a time, add the water to create a dough. Season with salt and black pepper.

3. Lightly flour your hands and evenly divide the dough into 8 portions. Roll the dough between the palms of your hands into 8 balls.

4. Transfer the balls to the refrigerator until needed.

5. Add the dumplings to your stew approximately 20 minutes before your stew is done cooking.

6. Using a spoon, place the dumplings on top of the stew and cover with a lid.

7. Continue to cook until the dumplings have fully risen.

8. Serve and enjoy.

Thanksgiving Leftover Dumplings

Not sure what to do with those all-important leftovers? No problem! These tasty dumplings are sure to tick all the boxes.

Servings: N/A*

Total Time: 40mins

Ingredients:

- Nonstick cooking spray
- Wonton wrappers
- Leftover stuffing (cooked)

- Leftover roast turkey (cooked)
- 1 cup cranberry sauce
- 1 chipotle pepper in adobo (finely chopped)
- 1 tsp adobo sauce

Directions:

1. Preheat the main oven to 350 degrees F. Using parchment paper line, a rimmed baking pan. Lightly spritz the paper with nonstick cooking spray.

2. Lay 1 wonton wrapper on a clean worktop.

3. Spoon approximately 1 teaspoon of the leftover stuffing along with a small piece of leftover turkey onto the middle of each wrapper.

4. Gently press the stuffing and turkey together to keep it in the center of the wrapper.

5. Dip your finger in a bowl of cold water and run it along all sides of the wonton wrapper.

6. Bring all sides of the wrapper up and over to enclose the filling and press gently together to form a purse shape.

7. Repeat the process with the remaining wrappers, stuffing, and turkey.

8. Lightly spritz the dumpling with nonstick cooking spray.

9. Transfer the dumplings to the oven and bake until golden brown for 12-15 minutes until golden.

10. In the meantime, in a bowl, stir the cranberry sauce with the chipotle pepper and adobo sauce.

11. Enjoy the dumpling with the homemade dip.

*Cook's Note: The serving size will depend on the quantities of your leftover ingredient

Turkish Manti Dumplings

Manti is the Turkish word for dumplings and consists of pasta filled with spicy ground beef, topped with a garlic and yogurt sauce.

Servings: 4

Total Time: 1hour 30mins

Ingredients:

Dough:

- 2 cups flour
- ½ tsp salt
- 2 medium-size eggs
- ½ tsp water
- 1 onion (peeled and shredded)
- ½ pound ground beef
- Salt and black pepper (to season)
- 3 tbsp vegetable oil
- 1 tbsp red pepper flakes
- 1 tbsp garlic (peeled and minced)
- 1 (8 ounce) carton plain yogurt

Directions:

1. In a mixing bowl, combine the flour with the salt.

2. Add the eggs to the bowl along with the water and using your hands to combine. You may need to add additional water as needed to create a soft dough.

3. Cover the bowl and set to one side for a minimum of half an hour.

4. Add the shredded onions to a colander and set over a mixing bowl. Drain their juice and discard.

5. Combine the onion with the beef, salt, and black pepper and mix using a spoon to mash.

6. Divide the dough into 2 even-size portions.

7. Lightly flour a clean worktop.

8. Keep 1 piece of your dough covered with a clean tea towel while you roll the remaining second piece of dough into a rectangular shape. Roll the dough as thin as possible. Using a pastry wheel or knife, cut the rectangle into 2" square.

9. Spoon approximately 2 teaspoons of the filling into the middle of each dough square.

10. Gather up the edges of the dough and pinch them together to form a beggar's purse shape.

11. Transfer the dumplings to a floured plate and scatter with more flour; this will help to prevent them from sticking.

12. Repeat the process with the remaining piece of dough.

13. Over low heat, and in a small frying pan, heat the oil along with the red pepper flakes. Take care not to burn the flakes.

14. As soon as the red pepper has begun to color the oil remove them from the heat and set aside to keep warm.

15. Stir the minced garlic into the plain yogurt and put aside.

16. Over moderately high heat, bring a large pan of salty water to boil.

17. Cook the dumplings until the dough is tender, for between 20-25 minutes. Drain.

18. Transfer the dumplings to individual plates.

19. Pour over the yogurt sauce and drizzle over the homemade hot, red pepper flake oil.

Sweet Dumplings

Amish Apple Dumplings

Still popular in Amish communities, these apple dumplings will have everyone coming back for more, and more, and more!

Servings: 6

Total Time: 50mins

Ingredients:

- 2½ tsp baking powder
- 2 cups all-purpose flour
- ½ tsp salt
- ⅔ cup butter (softened)

- ½ cup milk
- 6 apples (peeled and cored)
- 2 cups brown sugar
- 2 cups water
- ¼ cup butter
- ½ tsp cinnamon

Directions:

1. In a bowl, combine the baking powder, flour, and salt.

2. Add the butter and mix to combine.

3. Pour in the milk and mix until a soft dough form.

4. Evenly divide the dough into 6 even-sized balls.

5. Roll out each dough ball on a clean, floured worktop.

6. Place an apple in the middle of each piece of dough.

7. Fold the dough around the apple and press together to create a ball.

8. Lightly spritz a 9x13" pan with nonstick cooking spray.

9. Arrange the dumpling in the prepared baking pan.

10. Preheat the main oven to 350 degrees F.

11. Over moderate to low heat, in a small pan, combine the sugar with the water, butter, and cinnamon. Heat the mixture until it is just beginning to boil. Do this while frequently stirring.

12. Pour the sugar-cinnamon mixture over the top of the dumplings.

13. Bake in the preheated oven for half an hour, or until the apples are softened and the dough is golden.

Arabian Sweet Dumplings

This tasty dessert is very popular among the Arabian countries such as Lebanon, Egypt, Jordan, and Syria thanks to fragrant spices such as cardamom and saffron.

Servings: 25

Total Time: 35mins

Ingredients:

- 1¼ cups warm water
- ½ tsp ground cardamom
- ½ tsp saffron

- 2 cups all-purpose flour
- Pinch kosher salt
- 1 tsp dry yeast
- 1½ tsp granulated sugar
- 5 tbsp mashed potato
- Sunflower oil (for deep frying)
- Syrup, optional (warm)

Directions:

1. To a ¼ cup of warm water, add the cardamom and saffron. Set to one side.

2. In a second bowl, combine the all-purpose flour and salt. Set to one side.

3. Add the yeast and granulated sugar to ¾ of a cup of warm water. Allow to sit for 5 minutes.

4. Add the spice mixture and mashed potato to the flour and stir until combined. Next, add the yeast mixture a little at a time until combined. Continue to stir until the mixture resembles cake batter.

5. Leave the dough to double in size; this will take approximately 30-40 minutes. After this time, the dough should be bouncy and bubbly.

6. Heat sunflower oil in a medium-deep saucepan, Drop a teaspoon of batter into the oil, if it floats very quickly, the oil is too hot.

7. Drop ½ tablespoonfuls of batter into the oil and cook for approximately 60 seconds before using a wooden spoon to move the dumplings around. This will help them to cook evenly.

8. When the dumplings are golden brown, take them out of the oil and set them on a plate covered with kitchen paper.

9. Serve warm drizzled with syrup if desired.

Austrian Apricot Topfen Dumplings

Traditional Austrian topfen, or quark dumplings, are a popular summer dish dating back centuries. Here, they are prepared with a sweet apricot filling.

Servings: 18

Total Time: 1hour 30mins

Ingredients:

Dough:

- 3½ ounces butter (at room temperature)
- 2 eggs

- 18 ounces quark or curd cheese
- 1 tsp vanilla essence
- 1 tbsp granulated sugar
- 2 cups flour
- Pinch of salt

Filling:

- 16-20 small, ripe apricots
- 16-20 cubes sugar

Coating:

- 5 tablespoons butter
- 10½ ounces dry breadcrumbs
- 2 tbsp granulated sugar
- Confectioner's sugar (to serve)

Directions:

1. For the dough: In a bowl, combine the butter with the eggs using a hand mixer. The mixture may appear curdled at this stage.

2. Add the quark along with the vanilla essence, sugar, flour and salt, and mix to incorporate. Cover the dough with

kitchen wrap and transfer to the fridge for a minimum of 3 hours.

3. Wash and dry the apricots, slit one side of each apricot open, and take out the pit. Replace the pit with a cube of sugar and gently press the apricot closed.

4. Shape the dumplings: With well-floured hands and using a soup spoon, scoop out a liberal amount of dough. Flatten the dough with your hands and place an apricot, cut side facing downwards on the dough. Wrap the dough around the apricot, making sure you seal the edges. At this point, the seam should not be visible. Gently shape each dumpling into a round ball. Transfer the dumplings onto a platter and keep chilled.

5. For the coating: In a frying pan, melt the butter. Toast the breadcrumbs while frequently stirring and making sure you don't burn them. Remove the breadcrumbs from the heat. Stir in the sugar.

6. In a wide pot, bring lightly salted water to boil.

7. Turn the heat down and using a slotted spoon, place the dumplings into the simmering water. You will need to gently

nudge the dumplings with a spoon to make sure they don't stick on the bottom of the pot.

8. Once the dumplings rise to the surface of the water, cook for another 10 minutes, until the fruit inside is cooked through.

9. With a slotted spoon, remove the dumplings from the pot and roll them in the toasted breadcrumbs to evenly coat.

10. Repeat the process until all of the dumplings are cooked.

11. Serve with confectioner's sugar and enjoy.

Blueberry Pierogi

Pierogi are a classic Polish dish and they can feature sweet or savory fillings, Here, blueberries take pride of place to deliver a berrylicious dessert or snack to serve with whipped cream.

Servings: 6

Total Time: 1hour 20mins

Ingredients:

- 2 cups plain, all-purpose flour
- 1 tbsp icing sugar
- 1 whole egg + 1 yolk (lightly beaten together)
- 1 + cups warm water
- 1 pound 2 ounces fresh blueberries
- Vanilla sugar (to dust)
- 1 cup double cream, lightly whipped (to serve)

Directions:

1. Sift the flour along with the icing sugar onto a clean work surface.

2. Make a well in the middle of the flour.

3. Pour the eggs into the well, along with a few tablespoonfuls of warm water.

4. With a knife, mix to combine, adding more water 1 tablespoon at a time. The dough will be sticky and soft at this stage. Using your fingers, bring the dough into a ball.

5. Once the dough starts to come together, quickly knead the dough onto a floured worktop for 5 minutes, until elastic. If the dough is a bit wet, add more flour.

6. Transfer the dough ball into a bowl and cover with a damp clean cloth for 60 minutes.

7. When 60 minutes have gone by sprinkle flour onto a work surface.

8. Cut the dough into 2 pieces and roll the dough out to a (0.39") thickness.

9. Using a 3" pastry cutter cut circles out of the dough.

10. Repeat the process until all of the dough is used.

11. Cover the dough circles with a damp, clean tea towel until you are ready to begin filling.

12. When you are ready to fill, place a dough circle in the palm of your hand. Place 3-4 blueberries in the middle and fold the dough over the filling, in half to create a half-moon that covers the berries.

13. Carefully pinch the dough along the half-moon to seal.

14. Arrange the pierogi in neat rows on a lightly flour-dusted chopping board. Cover with a damp, clean tea towel while you assemble the remaining pierogi.

15. Bring a large pot of water to boil.

16. Using a slotted spoon, lower the dumplings one at a time into the water. Maintain the water at a gentle boil. The pierogi are sufficiently cooked once they float to the surface of the water; this will take a few minutes. Drain the pierogi and put to one side.

17. Serve while warm with a dusting of vanilla sugar and a dollop of whipped cream.

Canadian Boiled Dumplings

This classic native Canadian sweet treat is made using raisins and molasses. It is usually sliced and served as is, or with a knob of butter. Either way, it's a delicious dessert.

Servings: 20

Total Time: 4hours 5mins

Ingredients:

- 8 cups all-purpose flour
- 1 cup white sugar
- 2 tbsp baking powder

- 1 tsp salt
- 1 (15 ounce) packet raisins
- 12 fluid ounces evaporated milk
- 2 cups dark molasses
- 1 tsp vanilla essence
- ¾ cup lard (melted)

Directions:

1. In a bowl, stir the flour with the sugar, baking powder, salt, and raisins.

2. In a second bowl, whisk the milk together with the molasses and vanilla essence, and put to one side.

3. Using clean hands, work the lard into the flour-raisin mixture until a coarse-crumbly consistency.

4. Stir in the molasses mixture to achieve a wet and sticky dough.

5. Position a heatproof ceramic plate in the bottom of a large-size pan and fill with cold water. Over high heat, bring to boil.

6. Scrape the dough into the middle of a clean 2x2' clean cotton cloth. Bring the sides and corners of the cloth around the dough to create a beggar's purse shape. Tie the purse with a piece of strong kitchen twine, allowing approximately 1½" of room to allow the dough to expand.

7. Using a slotted spoon carefully place the dumplings in the boiling water, to immerse. Cover and return to boil. Turn the heat down to moderate-low and gently simmer for approximately 3½ hours.

8. Again, using a slotted spoon remove the dumplings from the water.

9. Remove the cloth and allow the dumplings to cool on a plate before serving either warm or cold.

Chinese New Year Dumplings

Yuanxiao dumplings are a big part of any traditional Chinese New Year celebration. Chewy and soft with a sweet, nutty filling, they're perfect for any special occasion.

Servings: 6

Total Time: 1hour 30mins

Ingredients:

- 2 ounces sesame seeds
- 2 ounces ground almonds
- 2 ounces ground walnuts

- ½ cup granulated sugar
- 1 tbsp vegetable shortening
- 2 tbsp water
- 1 pound glutinous rice flour
- Water

Directions:

1. Toast the sesame seeds in a small skillet over low heat for a few minutes; shake the pan continually to prevent burning.

2. Transfer the toasted sesame seeds to a food processor and grind to a fine-sand texture.

3. Combine the ground sesame seeds, almonds, walnuts, granulated sugar, and vegetable shortening. When combined, add a couple of tablespoonfuls of water to make the mixture moist enough to roll.

4. Spread half of the rice flour in a ¼" layer in a high-sided tray.

5. Roll the nut mixture into ½" wide balls and place on top of the flour in the tray.

6. Tip and shake the tray, so the balls roll around in the flour and get an even, light coating.

7. Transfer the coated balls to a second tray and sprinkle with water until well moistened.

8. Sprinkle the remaining rice flour onto the first tray and return the dumplings to the first tray. Shake and tilt the tray as before. Repeat this process until all of the flour is stuck to the dumplings. This may need up to 10 cycles to achieve.

9. Bring a large pot of water to a boil over high heat. Drop the dumplings into the boiling water. Nudge with a wooden spoon to prevent sticking. When the dumplings float to the surface, add 1 cup of cold water to the pot and cook for another few minutes.

10. Take the dumplings out of the pot using a slotted spoon and transfer to a platter. Spoon a few ladlefuls of cooking water over the balls to prevent sticking.

11. Divide the dumplings between serving bowls and serve straight away.

Dampfnudel with Vanilla Sauce

These Bavarian baked dumplings are poached in sweet milk with butter and vanilla. The German word Dampf translates as steam.

Servings: 9

Total Time: 2hours 5mins

Ingredients:

Dumplings:

- ½ cup milk
- 2 cups flour
- ½ package yeast
- 1 tbsp granulated sugar
- 1 tsp lemon zest (grated and chopped)
- 1 medium-size egg
- 1 tsp salt

Poaching liquid:

- 1 vanilla bean
- ½ cup milk
- 2 tbsp butter (melted)
- 2 tbsp sugar
- Vanilla sauce:
- 1 vanilla bean
- 4 cups milk
- 1 box vanilla pudding mix
- Nutmeg (to garnish)

Directions:

1. Heat the milk in a pan to scalding point. Allow to cool to 100-110 degrees F.

2. Add the flour to a bowl and pour in the milk. Add the yeast and sugar, mix to combine and set aside to sit for half an hour or until foamy.

3. Add the lemon zest to the milk along with the egg and salt.

4. Mix up the dough and set aside to sit in the bowl. Cover the bowl and set aside to rest for 60 minutes.

5. Punch the dough down and cut into 9 evenly-sized balls.

6. Preheat the main oven to 400 degrees F.

7. Transfer the dough balls to a baking pan and set aside to allow the dough to double in size.

8. Next, prepare the poaching liquid. Slit the vanilla bean and carefully scrape out the seeds. Add to the milk, melted butter, and sugar.

9. Pour in the poaching liquid and bake the dumplings on the lowest rack in the oven, covered, for 20 minutes. Do not open the oven during this time.

10. Uncover and bake for an additional 10-15 minutes until gently browned and the bottom crispy.

11. For the vanilla sauce: Simmer the vanilla bean in the milk with the pudding mix. Simmer for between 6-10 minutes, until the mixture thickens. Ladle the mixture over the top of the dumplings.

12. Garnish with nutmeg and serve.

Fruit Dumplings

Svestkove Knedliky are a perfect example of Czech cuisine at its very best where they are served as a side, main or dessert.

Servings: 20

Total Time: 45

Ingredients:

- 2 tbsp butter (divided)
- 1 pound 2 ounces boiled potatoes (grated)
- 7¾ ounces coarse flour

- Pinch of salt
- 1 egg
- 1 pound 2 ounces plums (pitted)
- 2¾ ounces confectioner's sugar
- 2 ounces ground poppy seeds

Directions:

1. On the stove, prepare a pan of boiling water.

2. Dissolve 1 tablespoon of the butter in a pan and melt.

3. Add the grated potatoes, coarse flour, pinch of salt, 1 tablespoon of butter and the egg in a mixing bowl and mix to create a cohesive dough. You may need to add additional flour at this stage if the dough is overly sticky.

4. Shape and roll the dough out. Cut the dough into small pieces. The pieces should be large enough to accommodate the plums easily.

5. Flour and shape the pieces into a small pancake shape.

6. Add a plum in the middle of each pancake and wrap the dough around to create a round dumpling.

7. Add the dumplings to a pan of boiling water and cook for approximately 10 minutes.

8. Using a slotted spoon, remove the dumplings from the water and set aside to drain.

9. Pour the melted butter over the dumplings, scatter with confectioners sugar, and poppy seeds.

10. Cut in half, serve and enjoy.

Indian Coconut Dumplings

Sweet sticky rice dumplings infused with exotic spices and tropical coconut filling are a delicious and unique treat.

Servings: 6

Total Time: 1hour 30mins

Ingredients:

- ¾ cup jaggery (or substitute brown sugar)
- 1 cup fresh coconut (grated)

- ⅛ tsp ground nutmeg
- ¼ tsp saffron
- ¼ tsp ground cardamom
- 1 cup water
- 3 tsp ghee
- ¼ tsp salt
- 1 cup fine rice flour

Directions:

1. Grate the jaggery into a bowl.

2. Place a heavy pan over moderate heat, add the coconut and toast for 2 minutes.

3. To the coconut, add the jaggery, nutmeg, saffron, and cardamom. Turn the heat down low and cook for another couple of minutes. Stir well and set to one side.

4. Bring a cup of water to a boil in a medium-sized pot. Add a third of the ghee and salt and turn the heat down low. Add the rice flour and stir well with a spoon — cover and cook for 2-3 minutes.

5. Take off the heat and transfer the dough to a mixing bowl. Allow to cool.

6. Add another teaspoon of ghee to the dough and 2-4 tablespoonfuls of warm water, then knead the dough until it is moist and soft.

7. Roll the dough into 12-14 even-sized balls. They should be lemon sized.

8. Grease your hands with a little ghee. Flatten each dough ball a little and place 1-2 tsp of coconut filling in the center of the dough. Roll and seal the dough around the filling.

9. Heat a cup of water in a steamer pot. Arrange a steamer rack inside the pot and add 7-8 dumplings at a time and cover — Cook for 10 minutes on a low-moderate heat.

10. Cook the second batch of dumplings.

11. Allow the dumplings to cool on a rack before serving.

Loukoumades (Greek Honey Dumplings)

These Greek honey dumplings are deep-fried, puff perfection. They are traditionally served hot with warm honey and typically enjoyed throughout Greece, especially during the wintertime.

Servings: 36

Total Time: 1hour 15mins

Ingredients:

- 2 (¼ ounce) sachets active dry yeast
- 4 ounces water (105-115 degrees F)
- 8 ounces warmed milk (105-115 degrees F)
- 1 tsp salt
- ¼ cup sugar
- ½ cup unsalted butter (melted and cooled)
- 2 eggs (lightly beaten)
- 3 cups flour (well sifted)
- Vegetable oil (to fry)
- 8 ounces Greek thyme honey (to serve)
- Cinnamon (to serve)

Directions:

1. In a small-size bowl, sprinkle the yeast over the water and set aside to dissolve and soften for approximately 5 minutes.

2. In the meantime, add the milk, salt, and sugar to a large-size mixing bowl.

3. Stir the yeast mixture along with the butter and eggs into the mixing bowl and beat well to combine.

4. Gradually add the flour while continually beating until the batter is sticky, smooth, and thick. You may need to add additional flour to achieve this consistency. Cover the bowl with a clean cloth and set aside for half an hour to allow the dough to double in size. Stir, cover, and allow to rise for an additional 30 minutes.

5. Pour the oil into a pan to a depth of between 3-4" and heat to a temperature of 360 degrees F.

6. While the oil heats, pour the honey into a small pan and warm over very low heat.

7. Stir the batter thoroughly.

8. Using a tablespoon, drop the batter into the hot oil and cook while turning in the oil until the batter is golden and puffed all over for 2 minutes.

9. Using a slotted spoon, remove the Loukoumades from the pan and place on a plate lined with kitchen paper to briefly drain.

10. Arrange a layer of the Loukoumades on a serving platter, drizzle with the warmed honey, dust with cinnamon, and top with a second layer of loukoumades.

11. Repeat the process until all the loukoumades are assembled.

North American Maple Syrup Dumplings

Maple syrup is an entirely North American product, so what better way to showcase the USA's sweet success that with these sweet dumplings?

Servings: 6

Total Time: 45mins

Ingredients:

- 2 cup unbleached all-purpose flour
- ¼ cup sugar

- 2 tsp baking powder
- ¼ tsp salt
- ¼ cup unsalted butter (softened)
- 1 cup milk
- ½ tsp vanilla essence
- 1 cup water
- 1 (19 ounce) can maple syrup

Ice-cream (to serve, optional)

Directions:

1. In a mixing bowl, combine the flour, sugar, baking powder, and salt.

2. Using clean fingers, work the butter into the dry ingredients to create a coarse sand consistency.

3. Pour in the milk and add the vanilla essence, and with a wooden spoon, stir until the dough is smooth.

4. Put the maple syrup along with the water into a large pan and bring to boil.

5. Using 2 spoons, shape the dough into 12 balls; you will need to use approximately 2 tablespoons for each ball.

6. One by one, drop the balls into syrup mixture.

7. Cover and turn the heat down. Simmer for approximately 15 minutes.

8. Serve the dumplings with the hot syrup and a dollop of ice cream.

Peach Perfect Dumplings

Did you know that 56% of the USA's peach crop and 96% of all processed peaches are supplied by California?! Enjoy a taste of the Sunshine state with these delicious little fruity dumplings.

Servings: 4-6

Total Time: 35mins

Ingredients:

- 1 cup granulated sugar
- 1 tbsp salted butter (at room temperature)
- 2 cups water (hot)
- 2½ cups fresh peaches (stoned, sliced)
- 1 cup all-purpose flour
- ½ tsp kosher salt
- 2 tsp baking powder
- ½ cup whole milk
- Cinnamon sugar

Directions:

1. Combine the granulated sugar, salted butter, and hot water in a saucepan over moderate heat.

2. Add the fresh peaches and bring the mixture to a boil.

3. In the meantime, combine the all-purpose flour, salt, and baking powder in a bowl.

4. Stir the milk into the flour mixture until combined.

5. Take spoonfuls of the dough into the boiling fruit mixture until all of the dumpling dough is used.

6. Cover the pan and cook for approximately 20 minutes.

7. Divide the dumplings and fruit between serving bowls and sprinkle with cinnamon sugar.

8. Serve straight away.

Scottish Clootie Dumpling

Traditional clootie dumplings are a delicious and comforting taste of the past, and for many will hold warm memories of their grandmothers preparing them at the stove on cold winter afternoons.

Servings: 6

Total Time: 3hours 25mins

Ingredients:

- 4 ounces suet
- 8 ounces + 1 tbsp all-purpose flour

- 4 ounces oatmeal
- 4 ounces currants
- 4 ounces sultanas
- 3 ounces granulated sugar
- 1 tsp ground ginger
- 1 tsp ground cinnamon
- 1 tsp baking powder
- 1 tbsp golden syrup or light treacle
- 2 medium eggs (beaten lightly)
- 4 tbsp whole milk
- Boiling water
- Superfine sugar

Directions:

1. Rub the suet into 8 ounces of the flour.

2. To the suet and flour mixture, add the oatmeal, currants, sultanas, sugar, ginger, cinnamon, and baking powder. Stir well until combined.

3. Next, stir in the golden syrup and beaten egg, when incorporated, stir in the milk a splash at a time. The dough should be firm but not overmixed.

4. Place a muslin cloth in a clean sink and pour over boiling water. When the cloth is cool enough to touch, wring it dry.

5. Lay the cloth on your worktop and sprinkle with 1 tbsp all-purpose flour. Place the dough in the center of the cloth and gather up the edges and tie. Do not tie the cloth too tightly as the clootie needs some space to expand.

6. Arrange a small plate upside down in a large cooking pot and place the tied up clootie on top, cover with boiling water and a lid. Simmer for 3 hours and check back at intervals to ensure the water does not boil dry.

7. When the dumpling is cooked, remove it from the pot and then remove the cloth.

8. Preheat the main oven to 225 degrees F.

9. Sprinkle the dumpling with superfine sugar and then bake in the oven for half an hour until it forms a shiny skin.

10. Slice and serve the dumpling warm.

Sour Cherry Varenikis

This Ukranian treat is a winning combination of sweet and savory.

Servings: 20

Total Time: 1hour 5mins

Ingredients:

- 2½ cups all-purpose flour
- ½ tsp sea salt
- 1 tsp bicarbonate of soda
- ½ cup kefir

- 1 large-size egg
- 1 (14 ounce) can sour cherries
- 1 tbsp granulated sugar
- ½ tsp cornstarch
- 4 tbsp butter
- ½ cup sour cream (to serve)

Directions:

1. Add 2 cups of the flour into a large-size mixing bowl. Add the sea salt and bicarbonate of soda.

2. Whisk the kefir together with the egg in a small-size bowl. Make a well in the middle of the flour mixture and pour in the kefir mixture.

3. Knead the dough, add 1 tablespoon at a time, until the dough doesn't stick to your hands.

4. Form the dough into a ball and cover the bowl with a damp, clean tea towel. Set aside to rest for half an hour.

5. While the dough rests, prepare the sauce: Strain the canned cherries through a mesh sieve into a bowl. Set 1 cup of strained cherries aside to use for the filling.

6. Pour the cherry liquid from the can along with the remaining cherries into a small-size pan. Add the sugar along with the cornstarch and cook over moderate heat until thickened. Put to one side.

7. Once the dough is rested, lightly dust a clean work surface with flour. Roll the dough out into a long log shape.

8. Dust the log with flour and cut into 20 evenly-sized portions. Shape each portion into a disc before using a lightly floured rolling pin to roll out into 20 (3") circles.

9. Put 2-3 cherries into the middle of each circle.

10. Fold the dough into a half-moon to enclose the cherries. Pleat or pinch together to enclose and seal. The dough will be elastic so it may be necessary to re-stretch the pieces as you create the varenikis.

11. Bring a pan of salted water to a rolling boil.

12. Add the butter to a large-size mixing bowl.

13. Add one prepared vareniki into the salted water and boil for 1 minute.

14. Using a slotted spoon, remove the vareniki and test if the dough is sufficiently cooked through.

15. In batches, cook the remaining vareniki, straining from the pot, and transferring them in the mixing bowl to toss evenly with the butter.

16. When you are ready to serve, put the cooked vareniki on a serving platter and top with the sour cherry sauce and a dollop of sour cream.

South African Dumplings in Cinnamon Syrup

Souskluitjies, pure comfort food at its very best. These pillowy cinnamon dumplings in a sweetly spiced sauce are utterly indulgent.

Servings: 4

Total Time: 55mins

Ingredients:

- 4⅔ ounces all-purpose flour
- ¼ tsp salt
- ⅓ ounce baking powder
- 6 tbsp margarine
- 1 medium-size egg
- 3⅔ ounces milk
- Syrup:
- 17⅔ ounces boiling water
- ¾ ounce butter
- 4 tsp ground cinnamon
- 1 cup sugar

Directions:

1. Sift the flour, salt, and baking powder into a bowl.

2. Using clean fingertips, blend margarine until the mixture is a crumbled consistency.

3. In a bowl, beat the egg with the milk and mix into the flour mixture to create a soft cough. You may need to add a drop more milk to achieve your desired consistency.

4. Preheat the main oven to 220 degrees F.

5. Heat the water along with the ¾ ounce of butter to boiling. Drop spoonfuls of the dough mixture into the boiling water-butter mixture.

6. Put the lid on the pot and boil for 15 minutes. Do not remove the lid during this step.

7. Using a slotted spoon, remove the dumplings from the pot and transfer to an ovenproof glass bowl, complete with lid.

8. in a small bowl, combine the ground cinnamon with the sugar.

9. Scatter the dumplings with some of the cinnamon sugar.

10. Add the remaining cinnamon sugar to the water in the pot and bring to boil.

11. Pour the cinnamon syrup over the top of the dumplings. Place the lid on the pot and transfer to the preheated oven until you are ready to serve for a minimum of half an hour.

Printed in Great Britain
by Amazon

71094190R00081